MY VERY OWN CHANUKAH BOOK

by
Judyth Robbins Saypol
Madeline Wikler

For our parents —
Fay and Alfred Meyers
Shirley and Norman Robbins

As my fathers planted for me,
so do I plant for my children.

— Talmud, Taanit

Copyright © 1977 by KAR-BEN Copies. Revised Edition 1978.
Published by KAR-BEN Copies, 11713 Auth Lane, Silver Spring, Md. 20902 (301) 593-2563
Printed in the United States of America.
ISBN 0-930494-03-2

INTRODUCTION

Chanukah is a holiday that captures the interest and imagination of young children. Candles, dreidels, latkes, songs, and, of course, gifts, are concrete expressions of celebration to which children can relate.

We disagree with those who would minimize the celebration of Chanukah because it is a minor holiday in Jewish tradition. It is a minor holiday only in the sense that it is of post-Biblical origin. In Jewish homes, and often in synagogues, Chanukah has been a popular and joyous family celebration for generations. The phenomenon of Christmas in America has, no doubt, contributed to the widespread celebration of Chanukah. But the holiday customs of gelt, latkes, dreidels and songs are part of a cultural tradition inherited from Eastern Europe and beyond.

We see the popularity of Chanukah to be a strength on which we can build. The celebration of Chanukah, and the questions it may raise in children's minds, gives us another opportunity to explore Jewish history, tradition, and values with them.

My Very Own Chanukah Book is a *kol bo,* a multi-purpose book. It is not meant to be read to, or by, a child in one sitting.

We have told the story as simply and as accurately as possible, given the mixture of history, legend, and interpretation that has been handed down to us. We have included a compendium of candle-lighting rules and customs. There are songs and music—some old, some new.

Finally, we have presented a series of themes, one for each of the eight nights. They are not rituals to be enacted at the lighting of the candles. Rather, they are suggestions of 1) things to talk about—miracles, legends; 2) family projects—maps, family trees; 3) bits of history and tradition—gifts, gelt, and games; and 4) opportunities for values clarification—why be different?

The themes don't have to be dealt with in sequence. Feel free to skip around and/or save some for next year. You may find some topics too "heavy" for preschoolers, though we think most give enough food for thought to stimulate discussion among family members of all ages.

Like many of you, we have been distressed at the focus on gifts, gifts, gifts. *My Very Own Chanukah Book* is our way of encouraging a shift in emphasis. Chanukah can be something more.

J.R.S.
M.W.

CONTENTS

ACKNOWLEDGEMENTS

In gathering information for this book — our most difficult research project yet — we found three anthologies to be especially helpful, and we commend them to those of you who want to know more: The Hanukkah Anthology by Philip Goodman (JPS), The Complete Book of Hanukkah by Kinneret Chiel (Friendly House) (both include many Chanukah stories for children) and The Hanukkah Book by Mae Shafter Rockland (Shocken) (for arts and crafts do-it-yourselfers).

We are, as always, indebted to our husbands and children for their impatience through yet another book, and to our many friends who read through the interminable drafts, including and especially our Rebbe, Oscar Groner.

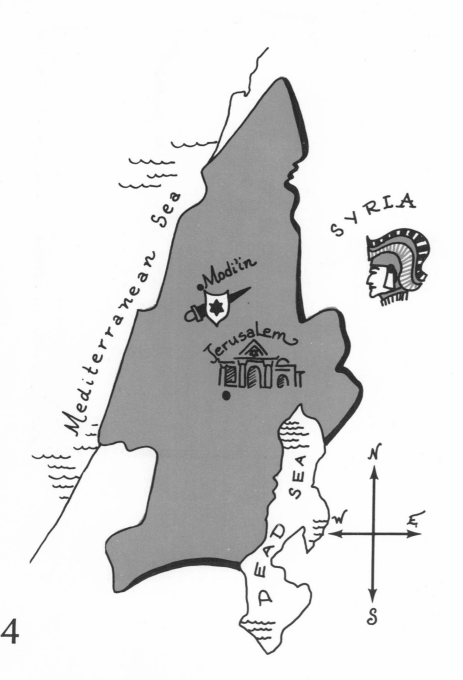

THE STORY OF CHANUKAH

Chanukah was first celebrated over 2,000 years ago. The Jewish people were living in the land of Israel, which in those days was called Judea. The capital and most holy city of Judea was Jerusalem. For many years, the Jews had worked hard to build a beautiful Temple there. On Shabbat and on the festivals, they came to the Temple to pray to God. They brought baskets filled with fruits, and other gifts, and put them on the Temple altar.

The Jews of Judea were not free. They were ruled by the King of Syria, a country nearby. For a time, the rulers of Syria let the Jews pray to God, celebrate Shabbat and the Jewish holidays, and follow the laws of the Torah.

4

Then a cruel King came to power. His name was Antiochus. He believed in the Greek religion, and he wanted everyone to believe as he did. The Greek religion was very different from the Jewish religion.

The Jews believed then, as they do now, in one God. The Greeks of long ago believed in many gods. They believed there was a god who made the sun shine, another who made the flowers grow, and still others who made it rain and thunder.

The Jews believe that you cannot see God, and that you cannot build statues or draw pictures of what you think God looks like. The Greeks believed they knew what their gods looked like, and they built statues, called idols, and prayed to them.

The Jews refused to follow the Greek religion.

5

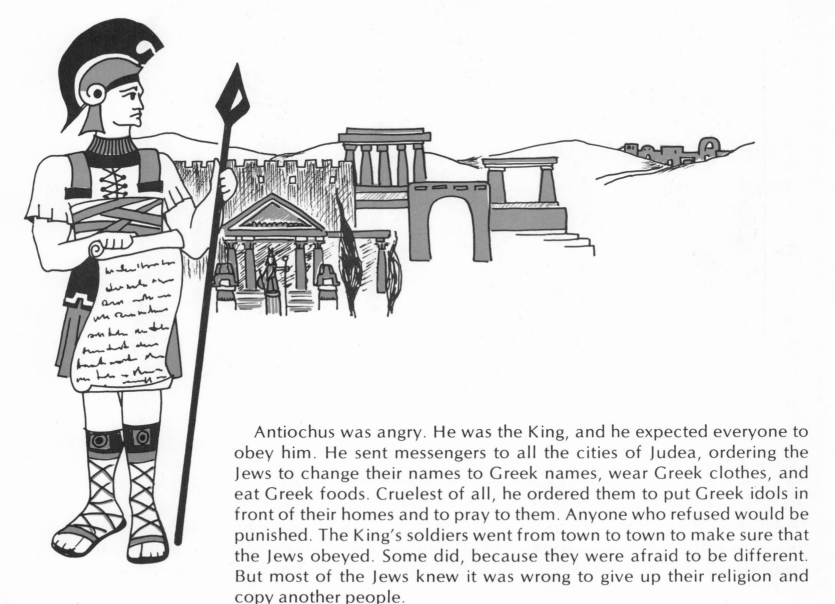

Antiochus was angry. He was the King, and he expected everyone to obey him. He sent messengers to all the cities of Judea, ordering the Jews to change their names to Greek names, wear Greek clothes, and eat Greek foods. Cruelest of all, he ordered them to put Greek idols in front of their homes and to pray to them. Anyone who refused would be punished. The King's soldiers went from town to town to make sure that the Jews obeyed. Some did, because they were afraid to be different. But most of the Jews knew it was wrong to give up their religion and copy another people.

6

Antiochus became very angry at the Jews who refused to change. He ordered his soldiers to march into Jerusalem. They destroyed homes and set fires in the streets. Many Jews were killed. Others ran to nearby villages. The soldiers entered the Temple. They tore down the Holy Ark and burned the Torah scrolls. They ripped the curtains and smashed the beautiful Menorah. They built a Greek idol and put it on the Temple altar. No longer could the Jews worship in their Temple.

7

In the town of Modi'in not far from Jerusalem, lived a Jewish man named Mattathias and his five sons: Jochanan, Simon, Judah, Eleazar and Jonathan. Because Mattathias was a wise and good man, he was the town's leader.

One day the King's soldiers came to Modi'in. They built an idol in the marketplace and called the Jews together to pray to it. Mattathias was called first. The soldiers ordered him to bow down to the idol. Mattathias came forward, but instead of bowing down, he raised his sword and turned to his sons and to the people of Modi'in. He told them that he would not stop believing in one God, and he would continue to obey the laws of the Torah. He called on those who wanted to remain Jews to follow him.

Mattathias, his five sons, and many of the Jews fought off the Syrians and ran away to the nearby mountains. They knew that to be free they would have to defeat the King and his army.

But Mattathias was old and sick. Before he died, he gathered his sons and blessed them.

"Chazak ve'amatz," he said to them in Hebrew. "Be strong and brave."

Mattathias appointed his son Judah to be the new leader. Judah was called "Maccabee" (which means "hammer"), and his army became known as the Maccabees.

It was hard for Judah to form an army. The Jewish people were not trained to fight. They were farmers, shepherds, and teachers. They had never been soldiers. They had no uniforms and few weapons.

But the small group of Jewish fighters knew the hills, caves, and countryside of Judea, so they were able to surprise the king's soldiers, even at night. Because they were a small army, they could move quickly. Most important, they were fighting for something they believed in. Their love for freedom gave them courage, and they fought long and hard.

The Maccabees went from town to town, defeating the Syrians and taking their weapons and uniforms. They broke the Greek idols in front of Jewish homes. King Antiochus sent more and more Syrian soldiers, but the Maccabees drove them away.

10

After three years of fighting, the Jewish army reached Jerusalem. They went first to the Holy Temple. Its walls were crumbling. Weeds were growing in the once beautiful courtyards. A Greek idol stood on the altar.

The Jewish fighters became builders. They scrubbed and polished the stone walls, fixed the doors and sewed new curtains. They cleaned the yards and planted new trees and flowers. They took away the idols and gathered stones to build a new altar. They found iron spikes and put small torches on them to make a new menorah.

Finally, they were ready to celebrate in the Holy Temple.

11

On the 25th day of the Hebrew month of *Kislev*, exactly three years after the Syrian soldiers had destroyed Jerusalem and the Temple, the Jews rekindled the lights of the menorah and rededicated the Temple. They celebrated joyfully for eight days.

There is a legend that tells that when the Jews searched for the special, pure oil needed to light the menorah, they were able to find only one jug, enough to burn for just one day. But the oil lasted and lasted, and the Menorah burned brightly for all eight days.

Judah the Maccabee and his brothers proclaimed that every year, beginning on the 25th of the month of *Kislev,* the Jews should celebrate a Festival of Lights for eight days. This holiday became known as Chanukah.

Chanukah means dedication—setting something aside for a special or holy purpose. The holiday of Chanukah celebrates the dedication of the Temple. The Maccabees cleaned and repaired the Temple and made it holy once again.

The holiday of Chanukah is also known as *Chag Ha'urim,* the Festival of Lights, and *Chag Hamaccabim,* the Festival of the Maccabees.

CANDLE-LIGHTING CUSTOMS

During Chanukah we read from the Torah and say special prayers in the synagogue. But the most important holiday ceremony is at home, where Jewish families light and bless the Chanukah candles each night.

There are certain rules for lighting the Menorah. Do you know them?

The Chanukah menorah—called the *Chanukiyah*—should be lit at sunset when the stars appear, and placed in front of a window, if possible, so that people passing by can see the candles burning and tell what night of Chanukah it is.

The Chanukah lights are for us to enjoy. They are not to be used for anything, even to light another light. That is why we have a special candle—the *shamash* or helping candle—which we use to light the others.

You need 44 candles for all eight nights. On the first night we light the *shamash* plus one, on the second night, the *shamash* plus two, and so on.

The Chanukah candles should be in an even row. No candle should be higher than any other candle, except for the *shamash*.

Candles should be lined up from right to left. But the last candle added is the first one lit, and the lighting continues from left to right.

Chanukah candles should burn for at least half an hour. You should not do any regular work (not even homework!) while they are burning. Just relax and have fun.

In some families it is the custom for everyone to light his or her own *Chanukiyah*. In other families, the parents and children take turns lighting the candles.

Because the menorah in the Temple was lit with oil, many families today light special oil menorahs. Although any oil may be used, a favorite is olive oil.

On Shabbat, you light the Chanukah candles before you light the Shabbat candles. If you have a *Havdallah* service at home at the end of Shabbat, Chanukah candles should be lit afterwards.

CANDLE-LIGHTING CEREMONY

We say two prayers each night when we light the menorah:
The first is a blessing over the special Chanukah lights:

בָּרוּךְ אַתָּה יְיָ אֱלֹהֵינוּ מֶלֶךְ הָעוֹלָם אֲשֶׁר קִדְּשָׁנוּ בְּמִצְוֹתָיו וְצִוָּנוּ לְהַדְלִיק נֵר שֶׁל חֲנֻכָּה:

Baruch atah adonai elohenu melech ha'olam asher kideshanu bemitzvotav vetzivanu lehadlik ner shel Chanukah.

The second blessing gives thanks for the miracles which have saved the Jewish people when others wanted to destroy them:

בָּרוּךְ אַתָּה יְיָ אֱלֹהֵינוּ מֶלֶךְ הָעוֹלָם שֶׁעָשָׂה נִסִּים לַאֲבוֹתֵינוּ בַּיָּמִים הָהֵם בַּזְּמַן הַזֶּה:

Baruch atah adonai elohenu melech ha'olam she'asah nisim la'avotenu bayamim hahem bazeman hazeh.

On the first night we add a third prayer giving thanks that our family and friends can be together to celebrate the holiday:

בָּרוּךְ אַתָּה יְיָ, אֱלֹהֵינוּ מֶלֶךְ הָעוֹלָם, שֶׁהֶחֱיָנוּ, וְקִיְּמָנוּ, וְהִגִּיעָנוּ לַזְּמַן הַזֶּה.

Baruch atah adonai elohenu melech ha'olam shehecheyanu vekiyemanu vehigi-anu lazeman hazeh.

After the candles are lit, it is fun to sing songs. Choose from those in this book or others you like.

WHAT IS A MIRACLE?

The four letters on the dreidel—*Nun, Gimmel, Hey* and *Shin* stand for the saying, *"Nes gadol hayah sham,*   A great miracle happened there."

What is a miracle? What miracles happened on Chanukah?

A miracle is a wonderful happening which doesn't seem possible. It is something we don't expect.

Chanukah is a celebration of miracles. Wonderful things happened which the Jewish people didn't expect.

First, even though the Maccabees were a very small army with few weapons and no uniforms, they were able to win over the very large, well-trained Syrian army. This was a miracle.

Second, there is the legend about why we celebrate Chanukah for eight days. The story is told that when the Maccabees had finished cleaning the Temple and were ready to light the Menorah, they were able to find only one jug of pure oil, enough oil to burn for a single day. But when they lit the Menorah, the oil burned for eight days. This, too, was a miracle!

Miracles—wonderful, unexpected things—happen in our day, too. Can you think of a miracle that happened to the Jewish people? Ask your family to tell you the story of how the State of Israel came into being. That was a modern miracle.

Can you think of any miracles that have happened to your family, or even to you?

15

WHAT IS A LEGEND?

A legend is a story about what might have happened a long, long time ago. Before people could read or write, and before there were books, stories were passed down from parents to children. Much like the children's game of "telephone," each time the stories were retold, things may have been added, changed or forgotten.

For a long time, the story of Chanukah was not written down. When it finally was, the writers did not remember everything that happened. Since that time, people have continued to ask questions about what took place. One important question they have asked is why we celebrate Chanukah for eight days. They began to think about why the number **eight** was chosen. These are some of the legends that have been told to explain why:

• When the Maccabees began to clean the Temple, they found that the Holy Menorah had been destroyed by the Syrians. So they gathered **eight** iron spears and stuck them in the ground to form a new menorah which they lit for the celebration.

• It took **eight** days to clean the Temple and prepare for the dedication.

• The jug of oil which should have burned for one day burned for **eight.**

• The Maccabees were so busy fighting the Syrians that they had no time to celebrate the fall holiday of Sukkot. When the battle was over, they dedicated the Temple and celebrated Sukkot for the usual **eight** days.

Another question people have asked is why Judah was called the Maccabee. Here are the legends that might explain why:

• Some say it is from the Hebrew word for hammer, *makav,* because Judah fought with the might of a hammer.

• Others say the Jewish soldiers carried banners with the Biblical phrase, *Mi chamochah ba'elim adonai,* meaning, "Who is like You among the gods, O Lord," The first letter of each of these Hebrew words spell Maccabee.

Which legends do you like best? Why do you like them best? Can you think of any other legends?

MAKING MAPS

When we read the story of Chanukah we learned that one of the reasons the Macca-bees' little army was able to win many fights was because they knew the hills and caves and countryside around Modi'in, and were able to surprise the Syrian soldiers.

Think about it. Pretend you invited a friend to play hide and seek with you. Your friend has never been to your house before. You know the special hiding places—in the garage, under the porch, behind a big tree. It will probably take your friend a long time to find you because he does not know your secret hiding places.

Draw a map of your street or neighborhood. Mark all of your favorite hiding places. Do you think you could be a good Maccabee soldier?

Here is a map of our street to give you some ideas.

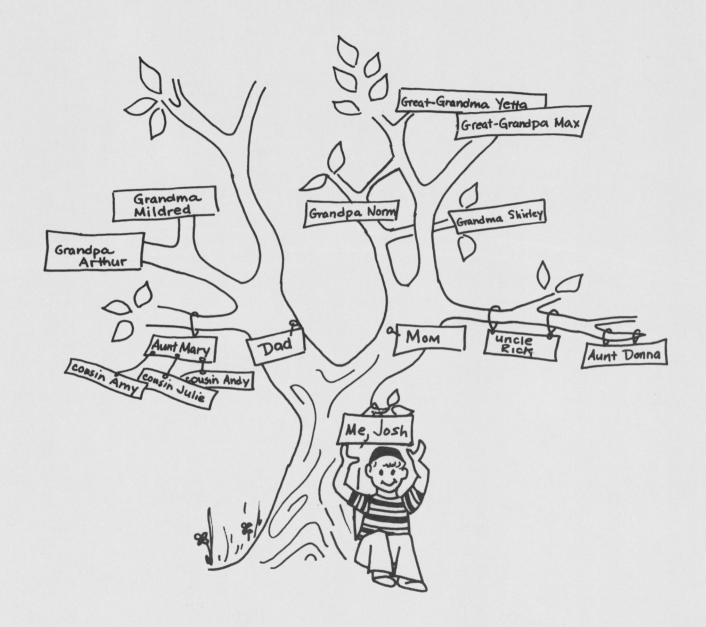

Great-Grandma Yetta

Great-Grandpa Max

Grandma Mildred

Grandpa Norm

Grandma Shirley

Grandpa Arthur

Aunt Mary

Dad

Mom

Uncle Rick

Aunt Donna

cousin Amy

cousin Julie

cousin Andy

Me, Josh

18

FAMILIES

The heroes of the Chanukah story are Mattathias and his five sons. Because Judah was captain of the army, we remember him best. But Judah couldn't have won the fight without help from his brothers—and their friends and neighbors.

Families are very important to us—not only our mothers, fathers, sisters, and brothers, but also grandparents, uncles, aunts, and cousins.

Years ago, many people lived with, or near, grandparents and other relatives. Today most children live with just their parents and brothers and sisters.

While the Chanukah candles are burning, why not talk about your family. How many relatives can you name? Who is the oldest? Who is the youngest? Where do your relatives live? Who lives the farthest away? Have you ever visited them? Do you ever send letters, drawings, or photos to let them know what you are doing?

What are some of the things that you enjoy doing with your family? Do your relatives get together to celebrate holidays? Have you ever had a family reunion?

Does your family have photo albums? Why not take them out and look through the old pictures. Do you remember when you were a baby? Are there pictures of your parents and grandparents when they were small? Ask them to tell you stories about how they celebrated Chanukah and other holidays when they were children.

You might enjoy making a family tree, a list of people in your family. Here is a sample of a family tree. Can you make one, too?

FREE TO BE

In many times and places, Jews, as well as other peoples, have had to fight for what they believed. Sometimes this meant war, and sometimes this meant escaping to countries where they could be free.

The Maccabees rose up against King Antiochus because he would not let them live as Jews. The Pilgrims came to America because the King of England would not let them practice their religion. Many Jews, too, came to America to escape rulers who would not let them live in peace. Members of your family—perhaps your grandparents, great-grandparents, aunts or uncles—may have been forced to run away from countries where Jews were not welcome.

Even today, some Jews are not free. There are Jews in Arab lands and in the Soviet Union who cannot celebrate Jewish holidays, pray in synagogues or go to Jewish schools. These Jews have shown great courage. Many of them have refused to give up being Jewish. They celebrate holidays and study Hebrew in secret. Though it can be dangerous, they continue to ask their government to let them go to Israel or another country where they can live openly as Jews.

When we feel joyful on the celebration of a Jewish holiday such as Chanukah, we should remember the Jews who are not as lucky as we are.

Some families light an extra menorah each night for a family who cannot celebrate Chanukah. Maybe your family would like to practice this custom, too.

The government of the Soviet Union has refused to allow most Jewish families to leave. These families are called "refuseniks." This Chanukah you might want to ask a grown-up —your parent, religious school teacher, or rabbi—to help you get the name of a refusenik family. You can learn the names of their children and become their penpal. They will be glad to get your letters. They will know that they are not alone, because you are thinking of them. This will give them courage.

FREE TO BE DIFFERENT

Being Jewish in the Maccabees' time meant being different. King Antiochus did not like people who were different. He ordered all the Jews to believe in the Greek religion. Many Jews obeyed the King because they were afraid to be different. But the Maccabees knew it was wrong to give up their religion and to copy another people.

Being Jewish today also means being different. We celebrate Shabbat, Rosh Hashanah, Pesach and the other Jewish holidays at home and in the synagogue. Our non-Jewish friends celebrate different holidays.

Around the same time we celebrate Chanukah, our Christian neighbors are celebrating Christmas, a very holy day in their religious year. Because there are many, many Christians, we notice Christmas a lot—in homes, shopping centers, on television and even in school. Even though no one is ordering us to give up our religion, at Christmas time especially, it can be hard for a Jewish person to be different.

- How do you feel about being Jewish at Christmas time?

- Do you ever wish you weren't different?

- Have you ever talked with your classmates or friends about Chanukah and other Jewish holidays? Do you feel proud to be a part of Jewish history?

- How do you think Judah Maccabee would have felt about being different if he were living as a Jew today?

GIFTS, GELT, AND GIVING

Exchanging Chanukah gifts has always been a part of the holiday celebration. Your grandparents will likely tell you that, when they were children, they received money—gelt—from their grandparents, aunts, and uncles. They used their Chanukah gelt for playing dreidel. Children with big families felt especially lucky because they were allowed to go from relative to relative collecting their coins.

Chanukah was also a time when parents gave gifts to their children's teachers.

The custom of tzedakah—helping those in need—was also traditional on Chanukah. Gifts of food and wine, especially latkes, were brought to needy families. Children often set aside some of the money they won playing dreidel to put in the family's tzedakah box. This money would be given to a charitable organization or used to buy trees in Israel.

Today, many school children give parties for people in hospitals and rest homes. Their gifts and songs bring happiness to those who cannot celebrate with their own families.

When you receive your Chanukah presents, remember to thank the people who gave them to you. Write a thank you note or draw a picture, and sign your name.

While it is fun to receive gifts, it is thoughtful to give gifts to those we love. Home-made things—cookies, pictures, decorations—are special, because the person will know you took time to make them yourself. Another welcome gift is a promise to do something helpful—keep the baby busy while mom is cooking dinner, make your own bed, or help set the table.

Giving tzedakah is also important on Chanukah. Plan to set aside some of your Chanukah gelt or allowance to put in the tzedakah box at home or school.

CHANUKAH IN ISRAEL

Chanukah is a grand celebration in Israel. From every Jewish home, office building, factory, school and synagogue, a menorah shines, growing brighter each night as another light is added.

Throughout the eight days—when Israeli children have school vacations—there are picnics, hikes, concerts, and parties.

The most exciting part of the celebration in Israel is the torch relay. On the first day of Chanukah, thousands of young people gather at Modi'in, the ancient home of the Maccabees. A large bonfire is lit. From the bonfire many torches are kindled. Runners carry these torches to every city and farm in Israel, stopping along the way to light the torches of other runners who will continue the relay. When the torch arrives at a city or town, the people gather to receive it and hold parades and large celebrations.

Torches from Modi'in are flown to the United States where they are relit and carried to synagogues and Jewish centers for Chanukah celebrations.

Why not have an Israeli Chanukah celebration? Even though it may be colder where you live than it is in Israel, it's fun to pack a winter picnic and bundle up for a hike in the woods. Don't forget the *sufganiyot* and hot cocoa for dessert!

23

CHANUKAH GAMES

The Chanukah lights are for us to enjoy. We should not do work while they are burning. For half an hour each night of Chanukah, we have time to play.

The most popular Chanukah game is dreidel. The dreidel is a spinning top. Its name in Yiddish means "turn." The Hebrew word for dreidel is *sevivon*.

There are four letters on the dreidel:

Nun   **Gimmel**   **Hey**   **Shin**

They stand for the words, *Nes Gadol Hayah Sham,* "A great miracle happened there."

Dreidels in Israel have the letters:

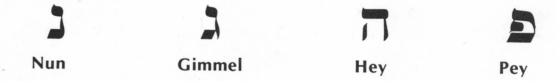

Nun   **Gimmel**   **Hey**   **Pey**

They stand for the words, *Nes Gadol Hayah Poh,* "A great miracle happened *here*!" Have you ever seen an Israeli dreidel?

Here are the rules for playing dreidel:

Everyone starts with an equal number of pennies, nuts or raisins. Each player puts one of these in the middle. The first player spins the dreidel. If it lands on:

Nun—the player does nothing
Gimmel—the player takes everything in the middle
Hey—the player takes half
Shin—the player puts one in

Before the next player spins, everyone puts another piece in the middle

People ask why we play dreidel on Chanukah. There is a legend that tells how the game might have begun. You will remember that cruel King Antiochus ordered the Jews not to study the Torah or observe Jewish holidays. But the Jews continued to do these things in secret. Whenever they were praying or reading the Torah, they kept dreidels in their pockets. If the Syrian soldiers knocked on their doors, the Jews hid their books and began to play dreidel. Thus they were able to fool the Syrians.

Many people play other games on Chanukah—chess, checkers, dominoes, cards, jacks, and board games.

Here is an idea for making your own Chanukah game:

CHANUKAH BINGO

You will need:
Squares of cardboard or poster board (about 10 inches square)
Paper or index cards
Crayons, markers, ruler, scissors
Buttons or pennies
Shoe box

Rule each card into nine boxes to look like a Bingo card. Draw Chanukah symbols in each square. Make each card different. (Some ideas are King, Judah, Star of David, Menorah, Shield, Temple, Dreidel, Candle, Latkes, Jug of Oil). You can use some of the same pictures on each card, but put them in different squares. Cut index cards or paper into small squares. Draw the same pictures or symbols on the smaller cards. Make sure you have a small card for each picture used on your Bingo cards. Put the small cards in a shoe box. One person is the caller. Everyone else has a large card. The caller picks a small card from the box, calls out the symbol, and whoever has that picture on his card, covers it with a button, penny or small cardboard circle. The winner is the first person to complete a row of pictures, either across, down or diagonally.

25

CHANUKAH FOODS

Most Jewish holidays have their own special foods and treats. On Chanukah it is customary to eat latkes *(levivot)* and doughnuts *(sufganiyot)*. Both of these foods are fried in oil and remind us of the miracle of the jug of oil that burned for eight days.

POTATO LATKES

Ingredients:
3 large potatoes (2 c. grated)
Small onion
2 eggs
2 tablespoons flour or matzah meal
1 teaspoon salt

Grate potatoes and place in bowl. Grate in onion. Add eggs, matzah meal and salt. Drain off excess liquid. Drop by spoonfuls into well oiled frying pan. Fry on both sides in hot oil. Serve with apple sauce or sour cream.

NO-PEEL LATKES

Ingredients:
1 egg
1 small onion quartered
3 c. unpeeled potatoes, cubed
2 tablespoons flour
1 tablespoon oil
1/4 teaspoon sugar
1/2 teaspoon salt
1/8 teaspoon pepper

Blend the egg and onion for a few seconds in a blender. Add half the potatoes. Blend until smooth. Add the other ingredients. Blend until smooth. Drop by spoonfuls into well oiled frying pan. Fry on both sides. Drain on paper towel. Serve with apple sauce or sour cream.

Doughnuts—sufganiyot—are the traditional Chanukah treat in Israel.

SUFGANIYOT

Ingredients:
3/4 c. orange juice or water
1/4 lb. margarine
4 Tbs. sugar
2 pkg. dry yeast
3 c. flour
2 eggs, beaten
Dash of salt

Combine orange juice, margarine and sugar and heat until margarine melts. Cool to lukewarm and add yeast. Stir until dissolved. Combine all ingredients and mix. Knead until smooth. (You may need to add more flour.) Place dough in greased bowl and cover. Let rise in a warm spot for a half hour. Punch down. Shape small pieces of dough into balls, rings or braids. Cover and let rise another half hour. Deep fry in hot oil. Drain. Put a few teaspoons of powdered sugar and cinnamon in a paper bag. Add doughnuts and shake.

A REMINDER: *Cooking with hot oil can be very dangerous. Make sure that a grown-up is helping you.*

BLESSINGS

TRADITIONAL

music arranged by: Sue Roemer

MA-OZ TSUR

TRADITIONAL

Ma - oz tzur ye shu - a - ti, L'cha-na-eh l'-sha be - ach.
Rock of a - ges, let our song Praise Thy sav-ing___ pow - er;

Ti - kon beit te - fi - la - ti v'sham to - dah ne - za be - ach.
Thou a - midst the rag - ing foes Wast our shelt'-ring___ tow - er.

Le-eit ta - chin mat - be - ach mi - tzar ham - na be - - ach,
Fu - rious they as - - sailed us, But Thine arm a - vailed_____ us,

Az eg - mor be - shir miz - mor, Cha - nu - kat ha - miz be - ach.
And Thy word___ broke their sword___ When our own strength failed___ us.

Az eg - mor be - shir miz - mor, Cha - nu - kat ha - miz be - ach.
And Thy word___ broke their sword___ When our own strength failed _ us.

28

CHAG HA-OR

words and melody by teachers,
College of Jewish Studies
Course: Music for Primary Level Teachers,
Fall, 1975   Sue Roemer, instructor

Slowly, Freely

1. I feel the warm can - dles glow, As we stand so near, The
2. We think a - bout the Mac - ca - bees, As we stand so near, They

flames are danc-ing in a row, Cha - nu - kah, Cha - nu - kah is here.
helped to keep our peo - ple free, Cha - nu - kah, Cha - nu - kah is here.

Faster, Rhythmical

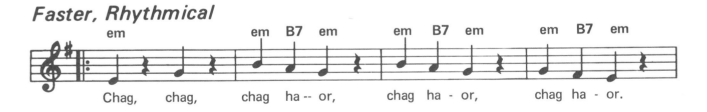

Chag, chag, chag ha -- or, chag ha - or, chag ha - or.

Chag, chag, chag ha - or, chag ha or. or.

AVI HIDLIK

TRADITIONAL

A - vi hid - lik____ ne - rot li ve - sha - mash li__ a - vu__
Fa - ther lit the can - dles for me, The sha - mash shone like a __

My mother gave me a levivah
A hot and tasty levivah.

kah, ve - sha - mash a - vu - kah, Yo - dim a - tem
torch, The__ sha - mash shone like a torch, Do you know what

(Refrain)
Do you know what it's for?
It's in honor of Chanukah.

My uncle bought me a sevivon
A top for me to spin.
(Refrain)

lich - vod mah, yo - dim a - tem lich - vod mah, yo - dim a - tem
it's for, do you know what it's for, do you know what

Li imi natnah levivah
Levivah chamah umetukah.

(Refrain)
Yodim atem lichvod mah?
Lichvod haChanukah.

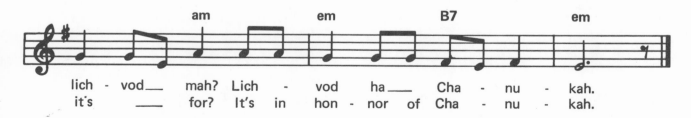

lich - vod__ mah? Lich - vod ha__ Cha - nu - kah.
it's __ for? It's in hon - nor of Cha - nu - kah.

Li dodi kanah sevivon
Sevivon mei-uferet yetzukah.
(Refrain)

30

OH CHANUKAH

Yiddish: M. Riversman
Hebrew: A. Evronin

FOLK SONG

Oh Cha-nu-kah, Oh Cha-nu-kah, come light the me-no-rah__, Lets__ have a par - ty, we'll all dance the ho - rah. Ga-ther round the ta - ble, we'll give you a treat: Drei - dels to play with and lat - kes to eat. And while we are play-ing, The can-dles are burn-ing__ low. One for each night, they will shed a sweet light to re-

1. mind us of days long a - go_____.

2. mind us of days long a - go.

Yemei haChanukah
Chanukat mikdashenu
Begil uvesimchah memalim et libenu
Layla vayom s'vivonen u yesov
Sufganiyot nochal bam larov
Ha-iru hadliku
Nerot chanukah rabim
Al hanisim ve-al hanifla-ot
Asher cholelu hamaccabim,

Oy Chanukah,
Oy Chanukah a yom tov a sheyner
A lustiger a frelacher
Nito noch a zoyner
Alle nacht in dreidlach shpiln mir
Zudig heyse latkes essen on a shir.
Geshvinder tzindt kinder
Di dininke lichtelach ohn
Zogt "Al hanisim," loibt Gott far di nisim
Un kumt gicher tantzen in kohn.

31